The Ultimate Guide to Eco-Friendly Living

Sustainable Solutions for Everyday Life

By Michelle Hoffmann

Table of Contents

Chapter 1: Introduction to Eco-Friendly Living.....................- 6 -

    The Growing Environmental Crisis ....- 7 -

    Defining Eco-Friendly Living.....................- 8 -

    The Ripple Effect of Individual Actions.....................- 9 -

    The Benefits of Eco-Friendly Living ....- 10 -

    Overcoming Obstacles to Sustainable Living.....................- 12 -

    How to Use This Guide ....- 13 -

    Getting Started.....................- 15 -

Chapter 2: Waste Reduction and Conscious Consumption ....- 16 -

    The Growing Problem of Waste ....- 17 -

    The Zero-Waste Lifestyle ....- 19 -

    Practical Tips for Reducing Waste ....- 20 -

    Conscious Consumerism: Supporting Ethical Brands .....- 25 -

    The Ripple Effect of Reducing Waste ....- 27 -

    The Path Forward ....- 28 -

Chapter 3: Energy Conservation at Home ....- 30 -

    Understanding the Impact of Energy Consumption ....- 31 -

    The Benefits of Energy Conservation ....- 33 -

    Energy-Efficient Home Practices ....- 35 -

    Sustainable Energy Choices: Renewable Energy ....- 41 -

    Creating an Energy-Efficient Future ....- 41 -

Chapter 4: Eco-Friendly Products and Alternatives.....................- 44 -

    The Growing Demand for Eco-Friendly Products ....- 45 -

    The Benefits of Choosing Eco-Friendly Products ....- 47 -

    Eco-Friendly Alternatives for Household Products ....- 49 -

    How to Make Eco-Friendly Choices.....................- 55 -

Chapter 5: Sustainable Fashion Choices .... - 59 -

The Environmental Impact of Fast Fashion .... - 60 -

The Benefits of Sustainable Fashion .... - 62 -

Key Principles of Sustainable Fashion .... - 64 -

The Rise of Circular Fashion .... - 70 -

Fashion for a Sustainable Future .... - 72 -

Chapter 6: Greener Food Choices .... - 73 -

The Environmental Impact of Food Production .... - 74 -

The Benefits of Sustainable Food Choices .... - 76 -

Practical Tips for Greener Food Choices .... - 78 -

Sustainable Eating for a Healthier Planet .... - 86 -

Chapter 7: Sustainable Transportation .... - 88 -

The Environmental Impact of Transportation .... - 89 -

The Benefits of Sustainable Transportation .... - 91 -

Sustainable Transportation Options .... - 92 -

The Future of Sustainable Transportation .... - 99 -

Driving Towards a Greener Future .... - 100 -

Chapter 8: Green Home Design and DIY Projects .... - 101 -

The Environmental Impact of Home Building and Renovation .... - 102 -

The Benefits of Green Home Design .... - 104 -

Key Principles of Green Home Design .... - 106 -

DIY Projects for a Greener Home .... - 113 -

Creating a Sustainable Home .... - 115 -

Chapter 9: Eco-Friendly Travel and Vacationing .... - 116 -

The Environmental Impact of Travel .... - 117 -

The Benefits of Eco-Friendly Travel .... - 119 -

Sustainable Travel Options .... - 121 -

Traveling Responsibly for a Sustainable Future .... - 128 -

Chapter 10: Building a Sustainable Future .... - 130 -

The Power of Individual Action .... - 131 -

How Small Actions Create Big Change .... - 133 -

Sustainable Communities: Building a Collective Future. - 135 -

Advocating for Policy Changes .... - 138 -

Education and Empowerment for a Greener World .... - 141 -

Creating a Legacy of Sustainability .... - 143 -

The Path to a Sustainable Future .... - 145 -

Living Sustainably for a Better Tomorrow .... - 146 -

Chapter 1: Introduction to Eco-Friendly Living

The Growing Environmental Crisis

As we move further into the 21st century, the world is grappling with an unprecedented environmental crisis. Climate change, deforestation, pollution, and depletion of natural resources are all symptoms of a system that has been unsustainable for far too long. Our choices, both big and small, have accumulated over the years, leading us to a tipping point where change is no longer optional—it is necessary.

While the situation may seem daunting, there is hope. We have the power to turn things around through the choices we make every day. Eco-friendly living is about rethinking how we interact with the environment and making conscious decisions that prioritize sustainability over convenience. By embracing small, consistent changes in our lifestyles, we can make a positive impact that collectively creates lasting change.

Defining Eco-Friendly Living

Eco-friendly living means making decisions that benefit the environment and help conserve natural resources for future generations. It is about adopting practices that reduce waste, minimize carbon footprints, conserve energy, and protect ecosystems. Sustainability is the core value of eco-friendly living—it's about meeting our needs without compromising the ability of future generations to meet theirs.

Living sustainably doesn't require radical lifestyle changes or extreme sacrifices. Rather, it involves being more mindful of our consumption, understanding the environmental impact of our choices, and committing to more sustainable alternatives in all areas of our lives. Whether it's using less plastic, conserving water, supporting local businesses, or making more responsible food choices, eco-friendly living is about making conscious decisions that reduce harm to the planet.

The Ripple Effect of Individual Actions

It's easy to feel as though individual actions don't make a difference in the grand scheme of things. However, the cumulative effect of millions of people making small, thoughtful changes can be profound. Every time you reduce waste, opt for sustainable products, or conserve energy, you are sending a message. That message encourages businesses, industries, and governments to take notice and follow suit.

Consider the growing trend of people choosing to reduce their use of single-use plastics. What began as a small movement among environmentally conscious individuals has now gained momentum, with large corporations, municipalities, and even countries introducing policies to ban or limit plastic use. This shift happened because millions of people decided to take action. It's a powerful reminder that individual decisions matter and can drive societal change.

The Benefits of Eco-Friendly Living

While the environmental benefits of adopting a sustainable lifestyle are obvious, there are also significant personal advantages. Living eco-friendly often leads to healthier living, both physically and mentally. Many eco-conscious practices, such as eating more plant-based foods, getting outside in nature, and reducing exposure to harmful chemicals, can improve your well-being.

Moreover, eco-friendly living can save you money in the long run. By choosing energy-efficient appliances, reducing waste, and buying fewer but more durable products, you can cut down on utility bills and spending. Additionally, when you make the effort to repair items rather than replacing them, you're not only reducing waste but also conserving financial resources.

In terms of societal impact, living sustainably helps create jobs in green industries, reduces pollution, and combats climate change. By shifting consumer behavior towards eco-friendly products and services, we send a signal to the market that sustainability is in demand, encouraging businesses to innovate and adopt more responsible practices.

Overcoming Obstacles to Sustainable Living

Many people feel overwhelmed by the idea of transitioning to an eco-friendly lifestyle. It's understandable—there is a lot of information to sift through, and it can be difficult to know where to start. Additionally, societal and economic structures often make it challenging to choose sustainable options. Eco-friendly products can be more expensive, and sustainable practices sometimes require more effort or time.

However, it's important to remember that perfection is not the goal. Sustainability is a journey, and every step counts. You don't have to transform your entire life overnight. Start small and build momentum over time. This book will guide you through easy and achievable steps to make eco-friendly living a part of your everyday routine.

How to Use This Guide

This book is designed to provide you with practical tools and strategies for living more sustainably, step by step. Each chapter focuses on a different aspect of eco-friendly living, from reducing waste to adopting sustainable fashion and food choices. The goal is to give you the knowledge and confidence to make more sustainable decisions in all areas of your life.

As you move through the chapters, you'll find tips that range from simple changes you can implement immediately, to deeper shifts that will take time but will yield significant long-term benefits. We'll cover everything from small habits that can reduce your daily environmental impact to larger lifestyle changes that have a broader effect. You'll also learn how to make eco-friendly choices without feeling like you're sacrificing convenience or enjoyment.

The beauty of eco-friendly living is that it is not a one-size-fits-all approach. It is a flexible, personalized journey that aligns with your values, needs, and circumstances. Some people may focus more on energy conservation, while others may prioritize reducing waste or supporting sustainable food practices. Whatever your priorities, the steps you take will contribute to a more sustainable and balanced world.

Getting Started

You've already taken the first step toward eco-friendly living by picking up this book. Now, let's begin the journey together. Start by reflecting on your current habits and identifying areas where you could make small, sustainable changes. Perhaps it's reducing your use of plastic, opting for energy-efficient light bulbs, or choosing to buy more locally sourced food. Whatever it may be, the important thing is to take that first step and build from there.

Throughout this book, you will find opportunities to reflect on your habits and track your progress. We encourage you to take action, set goals, and celebrate your successes along the way. Remember, every small change you make matters, and together, we can create a more sustainable future for our planet.

Chapter 2: Waste Reduction and Conscious Consumption

The Growing Problem of Waste

Waste is one of the most visible and pressing issues of our time. From overflowing landfills to polluted oceans, it is evident that our society's "throwaway" culture is wreaking havoc on the environment. In fact, it is estimated that the average person generates more than 4 pounds of waste per day, much of which ends up in landfills or incinerators. The effects are not only harmful to the planet but also to our health and quality of life.

Plastic waste is a particular concern. With its widespread use in packaging, single-use items, and convenience products, plastic has become a major pollutant. In the U.S. alone, over 100 million plastic bottles are used every day, many of which are discarded after a single use. Only a small percentage of these are recycled, and much of the rest ends up in oceans, rivers, and ecosystems, where it can take hundreds of years to break down.

The good news is that waste reduction is within our control. By making more conscious decisions about the products we buy and the waste we create, we can significantly reduce our environmental footprint and contribute to a cleaner, healthier world.

The Zero-Waste Lifestyle

One of the most effective approaches to reducing waste is the concept of zero waste. The zero-waste lifestyle encourages individuals and families to minimize the amount of waste they produce by rethinking consumption, reusing items, recycling, and composting. It's about living with intention and focusing on what you truly need—rather than mindlessly consuming goods that will only end up as waste.

Zero waste is not about achieving perfection; it's about making meaningful changes in your habits and reducing the amount of waste sent to landfills. Many people who adopt the zero-waste lifestyle find that it leads to more mindful living, increased satisfaction with fewer possessions, and even financial savings.

Practical Tips for Reducing Waste

There are many simple and effective ways to reduce waste in your everyday life. Below are some practical steps you can take to cut down on trash and adopt more sustainable habits:

1. Reduce Single-Use Plastics

The first step toward waste reduction is to limit single-use plastics, which are a major contributor to landfill waste and ocean pollution. Opt for reusable alternatives such as cloth bags, stainless steel straws, glass containers, and beeswax wraps. Choose products that are made with biodegradable or recyclable materials, and avoid products that are wrapped in plastic or have excessive packaging.

Tip: Keep a reusable water bottle, coffee cup, and shopping bags with you at all times. This simple habit can prevent hundreds of single-use plastic items from entering the waste stream.

2. Buy in Bulk

One of the best ways to reduce waste is to avoid buying products that come in individual, single-use packaging. Buying in bulk not only reduces packaging waste but can also save you money. Many stores now offer bulk bins for grains, beans, spices, and snacks, as well as reusable containers to fill with liquids like oil and vinegar.

Tip: Bring your own jars or reusable bags when shopping in bulk. This eliminates the need for plastic bags or containers that can be harmful to the environment.

3. Practice Conscious Consumption

Before making a purchase, ask yourself if you truly need the item, whether it's durable and reusable, and if there is a more eco-friendly alternative. Prioritize quality over quantity, and choose products that are built to last. By buying fewer, more durable items, you'll reduce the need for frequent replacements and waste generation.

Tip: Avoid impulse buys by waiting a day or two before making a purchase. This will give you time to evaluate whether the item aligns with your sustainability goals.

4. Repair and Upcycle

Instead of throwing away broken items or clothing, try to repair them first. Many items, from electronics to furniture, can be fixed with a little effort or a trip to a repair shop. Upcycling is another great way to reduce waste—take old materials or items and repurpose them into something new. Old furniture can be refinished, clothes can be turned into rags or new garments, and jars can be transformed into vases or storage containers.

Tip: Get creative with DIY projects. Websites like Pinterest and YouTube offer countless tutorials on how to upcycle and repair common household items.

5. Composting Organic Waste

Food waste is one of the largest contributors to landfill waste, where it decomposes anaerobically, producing methane—a potent greenhouse gas. Composting is a great way to divert organic waste from landfills while creating nutrient-rich soil for gardens. By composting fruit and vegetable scraps, coffee grounds, and yard waste, you can help reduce methane emissions and enrich the earth.

Tip: Start a composting system in your backyard or, if you live in an apartment, look for local composting services or community composting programs.

6. Recycle Properly

Recycling is a cornerstone of waste reduction, but it's only effective when done correctly. Many people unknowingly contaminate recycling bins by placing non-recyclable items inside. Be sure to familiarize yourself with local recycling guidelines, as they vary by region. Clean and separate recyclables such as paper, glass, aluminum, and plastics to ensure they are processed properly.

Tip: Set up a simple system in your home for sorting recyclables, compostable items, and trash. This can make it easier to stay on top of waste and ensure that recyclables don't end up in the wrong bin.

Conscious Consumerism: Supporting Ethical Brands

Reducing waste is closely tied to making conscious consumption choices. Instead of blindly supporting brands that prioritize convenience over sustainability, seek out companies that share your values. Ethical brands often offer products that are made from recycled or biodegradable materials, support fair labor practices, and have transparent supply chains.

When shopping, look for certifications that indicate a company's commitment to sustainability, such as Fair Trade, B Corp, or the Forest Stewardship Council (FSC). Supporting companies that prioritize environmental and social responsibility encourages the growth of the sustainable business sector and helps shift market demand toward eco-friendly products.

Tip: Research the brands you buy from. Many companies now provide transparency about their manufacturing processes, materials, and sustainability practices.

The Ripple Effect of Reducing Waste

The impact of reducing waste extends beyond the individual. When you make waste reduction a priority, you inspire others to do the same. Whether it's through word of mouth, social media, or community initiatives, the positive effects of waste reduction can spread far and wide. As more people embrace conscious consumption and waste reduction, businesses and policymakers will be encouraged to implement greener practices and reduce their own environmental impact.

In fact, communities that embrace zero-waste initiatives and recycling programs often see significant improvements in their environmental footprint. Schools, workplaces, and neighborhoods can come together to reduce waste through education, shared resources, and collective action.

The Path Forward

Reducing waste and practicing conscious consumption is a powerful way to live more sustainably. It begins with small changes that can quickly add up to a significant reduction in your environmental footprint. By committing to reuse, recycle, and purchase thoughtfully, you can play an integral role in mitigating the global waste crisis. Remember, every effort counts, and even small steps, like switching to a reusable shopping bag or composting food scraps, can make a big difference over time.

The journey toward waste reduction is not a destination but a continuous process of growth, learning, and adaptation. As you make more sustainable choices, you'll likely discover new ways to live with less waste and greater intention. In the following chapters, we'll explore other aspects of eco-friendly living, including energy conservation, sustainable fashion, and greener food choices, to help you build a life that's in harmony

with the planet.

Chapter 3: Energy Conservation at Home

Understanding the Impact of Energy Consumption

Energy consumption plays a significant role in our environmental footprint. The energy we use at home—whether for lighting, heating, cooling, or powering appliances—often comes from nonrenewable resources, such as coal, oil, and natural gas. The burning of these fossil fuels to generate electricity contributes to air pollution, climate change, and environmental degradation.

Globally, the residential sector accounts for a large portion of total energy use. In fact, households are responsible for about 20% of the energy consumed in the United States, with the average household using around 877 kWh per month. With the rising demand for energy and the urgent need to reduce carbon emissions, it's clear that energy conservation must be a priority in every home.

Fortunately, energy conservation doesn't require a complete overhaul of your lifestyle. By making informed decisions and adopting energy-efficient practices, you can significantly

reduce your energy consumption while saving money and

contributing to the fight against climate change.

The Benefits of Energy Conservation

Reducing energy use at home not only lowers your carbon footprint, but it also brings several other benefits. Some of the key advantages include:

- **Lower utility bills:** Energy-efficient practices often lead to lower electricity and gas bills. Simple changes such as using energy-efficient appliances, reducing heating and cooling needs, and optimizing lighting can result in significant savings over time.

- **Enhanced comfort:** Proper insulation and more efficient appliances create a more comfortable living environment, maintaining a consistent temperature year-round without over-reliance on heating and air conditioning systems.

- **Improved health and well-being:** By reducing the reliance on harmful fossil fuels, you are helping reduce air pollution, which can have serious health impacts.

Additionally, energy-saving strategies like using natural light can help improve the quality of your home environment.

- **Conservation of natural resources:** By cutting back on energy use, you reduce the demand for nonrenewable resources. This helps reduce the environmental toll caused by extraction, transportation, and burning of fossil fuels.

Energy-Efficient Home Practices

There are numerous ways to conserve energy at home, ranging from simple behavior changes to larger investments in energy-efficient technologies. Here are some of the most effective and practical strategies for reducing energy consumption:

1. Switch to Energy-Efficient Lighting

Lighting accounts for a significant portion of household energy use. Traditional incandescent light bulbs are highly inefficient, wasting about 90% of the energy they consume as heat. On the other hand, energy-efficient bulbs such as compact fluorescent lamps (CFLs) and light-emitting diode (LED) bulbs use a fraction of the energy and last much longer.

Tip: Replace your home's incandescent bulbs with LED or CFL bulbs. They use less electricity, have a longer lifespan, and reduce the need for frequent replacements.

2. Optimize Heating and Cooling

Heating and cooling systems are some of the largest energy consumers in a home. However, there are several ways to optimize these systems for maximum efficiency without sacrificing comfort.

- **Install a programmable thermostat:** A programmable thermostat allows you to set specific temperatures for different times of the day, ensuring your heating or cooling systems aren't running when not needed. For example, you can set the thermostat to lower the temperature while you're at work and raise it before you return home.

- **Seal air leaks:** Gaps and cracks around windows, doors, and ducts can cause your heating or cooling system to work harder, leading to wasted energy. Sealing these leaks with weatherstripping or caulking can improve energy efficiency.

- **Invest in insulation:** Proper insulation in your attic, walls, and floors helps maintain a stable temperature indoors, reducing the need for excessive heating or cooling.

- **Consider a high-efficiency HVAC system:** If you're due for an upgrade, consider investing in an energy-efficient heating and cooling system, such as one that uses a heat pump or geothermal energy. These systems can be more efficient than traditional air conditioning or heating units.

Tip: A ceiling fan can also help regulate temperature by circulating air. In the summer, use a fan to help cool the room, and in the winter, reverse the fan's direction to push warm air down.

3. Unplug Unused Electronics

Many electronic devices, even when turned off, still consume electricity. This phenomenon, known as "phantom load" or "vampire power," can add up over time. Devices like televisions, chargers, computers, and kitchen appliances continue to draw power when they are plugged in, even if they're not in use.

Tip: Unplug devices when they're not in use, or use a power strip with an on/off switch to easily disconnect multiple devices at once. This simple step can save significant energy over time.

4. Use Energy-Efficient Appliances

When it's time to replace old appliances, consider choosing energy-efficient models that have earned the ENERGY STAR label. These appliances use less energy to perform the same tasks, helping you conserve electricity and water while still delivering high performance. Energy-efficient washing machines, refrigerators, dishwashers, and water heaters can save hundreds of dollars annually in utility bills.

Tip: When shopping for new appliances, check the EnergyGuide label for information about energy usage and costs. This can help you compare products and choose the most efficient option.

5. Optimize Water Heating

Water heating accounts for about 18% of household energy use. Fortunately, there are several ways to conserve energy when it comes to heating water:

- **Lower your water heater temperature:** Setting your water heater to 120°F is sufficient for most households and can reduce energy consumption.

- **Insulate water pipes:** Insulating hot water pipes can help retain heat and reduce the energy required to keep water at the desired temperature.

- **Use low-flow fixtures:** Low-flow showerheads and faucets reduce the amount of water used, which in turn lowers the amount of energy needed to heat it.

Tip: If your water heater is more than 10 years old, consider upgrading to a more efficient model, such as a tankless water heater, which heats water on demand rather than storing it.

6. Consider Solar Energy

If you're looking for a larger investment to drastically reduce your energy consumption, consider installing solar panels on your home. Solar energy is a renewable, clean source of power that can significantly lower your reliance on traditional electricity. With falling installation costs and various incentive programs available, solar energy has become a viable option for many homeowners.

Tip: Research solar energy incentives and rebates in your area. Many governments and utility companies offer programs that can help offset the initial cost of installation.

Sustainable Energy Choices: Renewable Energy

In addition to reducing energy consumption, it's important to consider where your energy comes from. Many energy providers now offer renewable energy options, such as wind or solar power, which can significantly reduce your carbon footprint. Switching to a renewable energy plan can help support the growth of clean energy sources while reducing reliance on fossil fuels.

Tip: Check with your utility provider to see if renewable energy options are available in your area. Some utilities allow customers to choose a percentage of their electricity from renewable sources.

Creating an Energy-Efficient Future

Energy conservation is an essential part of living an eco-friendly lifestyle. By making small, consistent changes—such as switching to energy-efficient lighting, optimizing your heating and cooling systems, and using appliances responsibly—you can reduce your energy consumption, lower your utility bills, and contribute to a more sustainable future. As technology continues to advance, there will be even more opportunities to conserve energy and adopt renewable resources, making it easier than ever to live an eco-friendly life at home.

The key to success is persistence. Each small change you make, whether it's unplugging an appliance, choosing an energy-efficient lightbulb, or insulating your home, is an important step toward reducing your carbon footprint. As we continue to prioritize energy conservation in our daily lives, we can create a world that relies less on nonrenewable resources and moves toward a greener, more sustainable future.

Chapter 4: Eco-Friendly Products and Alternatives

The Growing Demand for Eco-Friendly Products

As awareness of environmental issues continues to grow, many consumers are turning to eco-friendly products as a way to reduce their environmental impact. Whether it's cleaning supplies, personal care items, or household goods, people are seeking alternatives that are made from sustainable materials, are biodegradable, and are free of harmful chemicals.

The conventional products we use daily—many of which are made from plastics, nonrenewable resources, or synthetic chemicals—can have a detrimental impact on the environment. For example, household cleaning products often contain toxic chemicals that can harm aquatic life when washed down the drain. Similarly, personal care items like shampoos, soaps, and cosmetics may contain microplastics or chemicals that pollute the environment and harm wildlife.

Fortunately, the market for eco-friendly alternatives has grown rapidly, and consumers now have access to a wide range of environmentally responsible products. By making the switch to

sustainable options, we can reduce our exposure to harmful

substances and help protect the planet for future generations.

The Benefits of Choosing Eco-Friendly Products

Choosing eco-friendly products offers several significant benefits. The most important of these is the reduction of harmful environmental impacts. Here are some of the key reasons to opt for sustainable alternatives:

- **Reduction of waste:** Many eco-friendly products, such as reusable containers and compostable packaging, help reduce the amount of waste that ends up in landfills or the ocean.

- **Conservation of resources:** Eco-friendly products are often made from renewable materials, such as bamboo, hemp, or organic cotton, which help conserve nonrenewable resources.

- **Reduction of harmful chemicals:** Many eco-friendly products are made with natural ingredients or non-toxic chemicals, which reduce the risk of harm to both human health and the environment.

- **Promotion of sustainability:** By supporting brands that prioritize sustainability, you help encourage more companies to adopt responsible practices and contribute to the growth of the green economy.

Choosing eco-friendly products is an empowering way to take control of your impact on the world. It also supports the growing movement toward more ethical business practices, where companies are held accountable for their environmental footprint and their contribution to sustainability.

Eco-Friendly Alternatives for Household Products

There are many areas in our daily lives where eco-friendly products can replace their conventional counterparts. Let's explore some of the most common categories and the sustainable alternatives available:

1. Cleaning Supplies

Traditional cleaning products often contain harmful chemicals that can pollute the air, water, and soil. In contrast, eco-friendly cleaning supplies are made from natural ingredients, such as vinegar, baking soda, essential oils, and plant-based surfactants, which are biodegradable and non-toxic. These products work just as well—if not better—than their chemical-laden counterparts while being safer for both your health and the environment.

Tip: You can make your own eco-friendly cleaning products at home using simple ingredients like vinegar, lemon juice, and baking soda. A mixture of vinegar and water can clean windows, while baking soda can be used to scrub surfaces.

2. Personal Care Products

Many traditional beauty and personal care products contain synthetic chemicals, preservatives, and microplastics that can harm the environment. Eco-friendly alternatives use natural ingredients, such as plant-based oils, shea butter, and essential oils, to nourish the skin without harmful effects.

Products like shampoo bars, biodegradable razors, and refillable deodorants are all excellent choices for reducing waste and supporting the environment. Many eco-friendly personal care brands also avoid animal testing and use ethically sourced ingredients.

Tip: Look for products with biodegradable or recyclable packaging, such as cardboard or glass containers. Avoid products with microbeads, which are small plastic particles

that pollute the oceans.

3. Reusable Kitchenware

The kitchen is one of the most wasteful areas in our homes,

with single-use plastic bags, cling film, and disposable

utensils being common culprits. By switching to reusable

alternatives, we can significantly reduce waste.

Some great eco-friendly options include:

- **Reusable food storage:** Beeswax wraps, silicone bags, and glass containers are excellent alternatives to plastic wrap and single-use plastic bags.

- **Compostable plates and utensils:** Instead of plastic plates and cutlery, choose products made from bamboo, cornstarch, or other biodegradable materials.

- **Sustainable cleaning cloths:** Instead of paper towels, opt for washable, reusable cloths made from organic cotton or bamboo.

Tip: Keep a set of reusable food wraps, cloth napkins, and stainless steel or bamboo straws in your kitchen to replace single-use items.

4. Sustainable Fashion

The fashion industry is one of the largest polluters in the world, responsible for massive water consumption, chemical use, and textile waste. Eco-friendly fashion focuses on using sustainable materials, such as organic cotton, hemp, wool, and recycled fabrics, and supporting ethical manufacturing processes that ensure fair wages and safe working conditions.

Brands that prioritize sustainable fashion often offer clothing that is designed to last longer, reducing the need for frequent replacements. Many also offer clothing recycling programs or use upcycled materials to create new garments.

Tip: Buy second-hand clothing or swap clothes with friends to reduce demand for new garments. When you do buy new items, look for brands that offer transparency about their supply chain and use eco-friendly materials.

5. Eco-Friendly Home Decor

When decorating your home, it's important to choose furnishings and accessories that are made from sustainable, non-toxic materials. Many home decor items are made from plastics or synthetics that contribute to pollution and environmental harm.

Look for furniture and decor made from sustainable wood, bamboo, recycled materials, or natural fibers. Many eco-friendly furniture makers also focus on minimizing waste and using responsible manufacturing processes.

Tip: Choose second-hand or vintage furniture to reduce the demand for new resources. This not only helps the environment but also adds a unique, personalized touch to your home.

How to Make Eco-Friendly Choices

Making the switch to eco-friendly products doesn't have to be overwhelming. Here are some simple strategies for incorporating sustainable alternatives into your daily life:

1. Start Small

You don't have to overhaul your entire home or lifestyle overnight. Start by replacing one product at a time. Perhaps begin by switching to a sustainable cleaning product or replacing your disposable plastic bags with reusable ones. As you become more familiar with eco-friendly alternatives, you can gradually make more sustainable choices in other areas.

2. Research Brands

Look for brands that align with your values. Many companies are transparent about their environmental and ethical practices, so take the time to research before making a purchase. Certifications such as Fair Trade, B Corp, and the

Global Organic Textile Standard (GOTS) can help you identify responsible brands.

3. Prioritize Quality Over Quantity

When it comes to eco-friendly products, quality often matters more than quantity. Choose durable, long-lasting items that will reduce the need for replacements. This is especially important for products like clothing, appliances, and furniture, where investing in quality can save both money and resources in the long run.

4. Buy Local

Supporting local businesses is another great way to reduce your environmental footprint. By purchasing locally made products, you can reduce the carbon footprint associated with transportation and support your local economy.

Empowering Change Through Conscious Consumption

By choosing eco-friendly products and alternatives, we are not only helping to protect the environment, but we are also empowering ourselves to make a positive impact. Each time we choose a sustainable product over its conventional counterpart, we contribute to the growth of a greener economy and encourage more companies to adopt responsible business practices.

Living an eco-friendly lifestyle requires thoughtful choices, but these choices do not need to be difficult or costly. In many cases, sustainable products are just as affordable and accessible as conventional ones, and they often offer additional benefits like improved health and long-term savings.

As you continue to make eco-friendly choices, remember that every step counts. Whether you're choosing natural cleaning supplies, investing in durable clothing, or reducing waste in your kitchen, each action contributes to a healthier planet for

future generations.

Chapter 5: Sustainable Fashion Choices

The Environmental Impact of Fast Fashion

Fashion is one of the most dynamic and influential industries globally, but it is also one of the most environmentally damaging. Fast fashion—the practice of producing inexpensive, trendy clothing at high volumes to meet ever-changing consumer demand—has become the norm in many parts of the world. While fast fashion allows consumers to stay on top of trends and buy clothing at low prices, it comes at a significant environmental cost.

The fast fashion industry is responsible for a large portion of global pollution, including high carbon emissions, water waste, and textile waste. The production of cheap, synthetic fabrics like polyester and nylon, which are derived from petroleum, contributes to the depletion of natural resources and releases microplastics into our oceans. Additionally, the dyeing process for textiles is water-intensive and can release harmful chemicals into water systems.

Another troubling aspect of fast fashion is the waste it generates. The constant production of low-cost, low-quality clothing leads to garments that are often discarded after only a few uses. It is estimated that nearly 85% of textiles are thrown away each year in the United States alone, and many of these garments end up in landfills where they can take hundreds of years to decompose.

The good news is that consumers have the power to shift the industry toward more sustainable practices. By making thoughtful fashion choices, we can reduce our environmental impact and support brands that prioritize ethics, sustainability, and responsible production.

The Benefits of Sustainable Fashion

Sustainable fashion is all about making clothing choices that are better for the environment, workers, and communities. The benefits of adopting a sustainable fashion mindset go beyond reducing waste—they also include promoting fair labor practices, conserving natural resources, and creating a circular economy where products are reused or recycled.

Here are some of the key benefits of sustainable fashion:

- **Reduction in environmental pollution:** By choosing materials that are biodegradable, organic, or recycled, we can significantly reduce the environmental impact of the fashion industry.

- **Conservation of natural resources:** Sustainable fashion prioritizes the use of renewable resources, such as organic cotton, hemp, and bamboo, which require fewer pesticides and water to grow.

- **Support for ethical practices:** Many sustainable brands focus on fair labor practices, ensuring that workers are paid fair wages and work in safe, healthy conditions.

- **Longer-lasting clothing:** High-quality, sustainably produced garments are made to last, reducing the need for constant replacements and lowering overall consumption.

Key Principles of Sustainable Fashion

Sustainable fashion can be approached in various ways, depending on your preferences and lifestyle. Here are some key principles to help guide your fashion choices:

1. Buy Less, Choose Wisely

One of the cornerstones of sustainable fashion is the concept of mindful consumption. Instead of buying clothing based on impulse or fleeting trends, focus on purchasing items that you truly need and will wear regularly. By making thoughtful purchases, you can reduce the volume of clothing you buy, thus decreasing the demand for mass-produced garments.

Tip: Before buying something new, ask yourself if it fits your personal style, if it will last a long time, and if you truly need it. If the answer is no, consider skipping the purchase.

2. Invest in Quality Over Quantity

Sustainable fashion emphasizes the importance of quality over quantity. High-quality, durable clothing tends to last longer than cheap, fast-fashion garments, which often fall apart after a few wears. By investing in well-made items, you can save money in the long term and reduce the need to constantly replace worn-out clothing.

Tip: Look for clothing made from natural fibers like organic cotton, wool, linen, or hemp, as these materials are often more durable and have a smaller environmental footprint than synthetic fabrics.

3. Choose Sustainable Fabrics

The fabrics used in clothing production can have a significant impact on the environment. Some fabrics, like polyester, nylon, and acrylic, are made from petroleum-based resources and release microplastics into the environment when washed. On the other hand, sustainable fabrics like organic cotton, Tencel, and recycled polyester are better for the environment.

Tip: Look for clothing made from natural fibers, like organic cotton, hemp, wool, and linen. These materials are biodegradable and typically require fewer chemicals and water to produce. Recycled fabrics are another great option, as they help reduce waste and conserve resources.

4. Support Ethical and Transparent Brands

Many sustainable fashion brands are committed to ethical production practices, including fair wages, safe working conditions, and the use of environmentally friendly materials. By supporting these brands, you help create a demand for ethical practices in the fashion industry.

Tip: Research the brands you buy from to ensure they align with your values. Look for certifications such as Fair Trade, Global Organic Textile Standard (GOTS), or B Corp, which indicate that the company prioritizes sustainability and ethical practices.

5. Embrace Second-Hand and Vintage Clothing

One of the best ways to reduce your fashion footprint is by buying second-hand or vintage clothing. Not only does this reduce the demand for new clothing, but it also gives pre-loved garments a second life. Thrift stores, consignment shops, and online platforms like Depop or Poshmark are excellent places to find unique, high-quality pieces at affordable prices.

Tip: Set aside time to explore second-hand stores or browse online resale platforms. You may be surprised by the treasures you can find, and you'll help reduce the demand for new clothing.

6. Upcycle and Repair Clothing

Instead of discarding clothes that no longer fit or have minor damage, consider upcycling or repairing them. Upcycling involves taking old clothing and turning it into something new, such as turning a worn-out shirt into a tote bag or creating a patchwork design on torn jeans. Many clothing repairs can be done at home with basic sewing skills, helping you extend the life of your garments.

Tip: Invest in basic sewing tools like needles, thread, and fabric patches to make simple repairs. Not only will this save your clothes from being thrown away, but it will also give you a chance to get creative.

7. Care for Your Clothes Properly

Proper care and maintenance can help extend the life of your clothing and reduce the need for frequent replacements. Washing clothes in cold water, air-drying instead of using a dryer, and avoiding frequent ironing can all help preserve the integrity of your garments.

Tip: Follow the care instructions on clothing labels to ensure that your items last longer. Additionally, consider washing clothes in a microfiber bag to capture microplastics that can

be released during laundry.

The Rise of Circular Fashion

One of the most promising trends in sustainable fashion is the rise of circular fashion. This model is based on the idea of creating a closed-loop system, where clothes are made to be reused, repaired, or recycled, rather than being discarded. Circular fashion seeks to eliminate waste by keeping materials in use for as long as possible, either by recycling old garments into new ones or by encouraging consumers to buy less and care for their clothing better.

Brands that embrace circular fashion often offer clothing repair services, recycling programs, or buy-back initiatives. Some companies even create garments made entirely from recycled materials, which can be recycled again at the end of their life cycle.

Tip: Look for brands that offer take-back programs or use circular fashion principles. Recycling your clothes helps reduce textile waste and supports a more sustainable fashion

industry.

Fashion for a Sustainable Future

The fashion industry's environmental impact is undeniable, but by making conscious, sustainable choices, we can collectively drive change. Sustainable fashion is about more than just reducing waste—it's about creating a system where clothes are made with respect for the environment, workers, and communities. By buying less, investing in quality, supporting ethical brands, and embracing second-hand shopping, we can all be part of the solution.

As you embrace sustainable fashion, remember that small, consistent changes can make a big difference. Whether you're opting for organic cotton, choosing second-hand items, or taking better care of your clothes, each choice helps reduce the environmental impact of the fashion industry. Together, we can create a more sustainable future—one stylish outfit at a time.

Chapter 6: Greener Food Choices

The Environmental Impact of Food Production

Our food choices have a significant impact on the environment. The process of growing, transporting, and consuming food involves the use of resources such as water, land, and energy. However, not all food production systems are created equal—some are far more resource-intensive and polluting than others.

Agriculture is responsible for about 25% of global greenhouse gas emissions, with livestock production contributing a large portion of these emissions due to methane released by animals like cows. In addition to greenhouse gases, conventional farming practices often lead to soil degradation, deforestation, and the contamination of water supplies with pesticides and fertilizers.

The transportation of food also contributes to its environmental footprint. Most of the food we consume is shipped across long distances, which requires large amounts of energy and results in significant carbon emissions. For

example, importing fruits and vegetables from other countries

increases the carbon footprint of the food compared to

purchasing locally grown produce.

By making more conscious food choices, we can significantly

reduce our environmental impact, promote biodiversity, and

support sustainable agricultural practices. Fortunately, there

are many simple ways to make greener food choices that

benefit both the planet and your health.

The Benefits of Sustainable Food Choices

Choosing more sustainable food options offers several advantages, both for the environment and for personal well-being. Here are some of the key benefits of greener food choices:

- **Reduced greenhouse gas emissions:** Sustainable food practices, such as eating more plant-based foods and buying locally grown produce, can reduce the greenhouse gas emissions associated with food production and transportation.

- **Conservation of natural resources:** By opting for food grown with fewer pesticides and chemical fertilizers, you help conserve soil and water, reducing the depletion of vital natural resources.

- **Improved health:** Many sustainable food choices, such as organic fruits and vegetables, whole grains, and plant-based proteins, are healthier for you and may lower the risk of chronic diseases like heart disease, diabetes, and cancer.

- **Support for ethical practices:** Sustainable food choices often support fair trade practices, which ensure that farmers are paid fair wages and work in safe, healthy conditions.

Making the shift to more sustainable eating habits doesn't require a complete overhaul of your diet. Simple changes, such as eating less meat, buying locally, and reducing food waste, can have a significant positive impact.

Practical Tips for Greener Food Choices

There are many ways to make your food choices more sustainable. Whether you're looking to reduce your environmental footprint, support local farmers, or make healthier choices, here are some practical tips for greening your diet:

1. Eat More Plant-Based Foods

One of the most effective ways to reduce your environmental impact is by eating more plant-based foods. Livestock farming requires large amounts of land, water, and feed, and it produces significant greenhouse gas emissions, especially from ruminant animals like cows and sheep. By choosing more plant-based meals, you can help reduce the demand for resource-intensive animal agriculture.

Plant-based foods like beans, lentils, whole grains, fruits, and vegetables are not only better for the planet, but they are also packed with essential nutrients. A plant-based diet is rich in fiber, antioxidants, and healthy fats, which can improve heart health, reduce inflammation, and lower the risk of chronic diseases.

Tip: Try incorporating "Meatless Mondays" into your weekly routine, or experiment with plant-based proteins like tofu, tempeh, or legumes in place of animal products.

2. Buy Locally Grown, Seasonal Produce

Purchasing locally grown food is one of the most impactful ways to reduce the environmental impact of your diet. Local food doesn't need to be transported over long distances, which cuts down on fuel use and carbon emissions. Additionally, buying seasonal produce ensures that the food is grown in its ideal climate, reducing the need for artificial climate control, pesticides, and fertilizers.

Farmers' markets, local co-ops, and community-supported agriculture (CSA) programs are great places to find fresh, locally grown produce. Not only do these options reduce your carbon footprint, but they also support local farmers and the regional economy.

Tip: Plan your meals around what is in season in your area. This not only supports local agriculture but also helps ensure that you're eating fresh, nutrient-dense foods.

3. Choose Organic When Possible

Organic farming practices focus on the use of natural fertilizers, crop rotations, and integrated pest management, which are better for the environment than conventional farming methods. Organic farming helps preserve soil health, reduces water pollution, and minimizes exposure to harmful pesticides and synthetic chemicals.

While organic food can sometimes be more expensive, it's an investment in both your health and the environment. When shopping for organic products, prioritize items that are commonly treated with pesticides, such as fruits, vegetables, and grains.

Tip: Look for organic certification labels on your food, and focus on purchasing organic products that are most likely to be contaminated with pesticides, such as apples, strawberries, and spinach.

4. Minimize Food Waste

Food waste is a massive problem globally. It's estimated that nearly one-third of all food produced for human consumption is lost or wasted each year. This waste contributes to unnecessary carbon emissions and squanders valuable resources like water, labor, and energy.

To reduce food waste, start by purchasing only what you need and using leftovers creatively. Plan your meals to avoid over-purchasing, and use storage techniques to keep perishable foods fresh for longer. If you do have leftover food, try freezing it for later use or composting it to reduce landfill waste.

Tip: Practice portion control by serving smaller portions and encouraging family members to finish their plates before serving more. Compost food scraps instead of throwing them away, creating nutrient-rich soil for your garden.

5. Support Sustainable Seafood

Seafood can be a great source of protein and healthy fats, but overfishing, unsustainable farming practices, and habitat destruction are serious environmental concerns. To make sustainable seafood choices, look for certifications such as the Marine Stewardship Council (MSC) label, which indicates that the fish was caught using sustainable practices.

If you eat farmed seafood, choose options that are raised in environmentally responsible ways. Some aquaculture operations are better than others at minimizing their environmental impact, so it's important to research the source of your seafood.

Tip: Opt for seafood species that are abundant and lower on the food chain, such as sardines, mackerel, or anchovies, as they are more sustainable and have a smaller environmental footprint.

6. Grow Your Own Food

Growing your own food is one of the most rewarding ways to ensure that you're eating sustainably. Whether you have a small garden, a balcony, or even just a few pots, growing your own vegetables and herbs reduces your reliance on store-bought produce, minimizes transportation emissions, and provides you with fresh, organic ingredients.

Even if you don't have a lot of space, you can grow easy-to-care-for crops like tomatoes, lettuce, herbs, or radishes. Container gardening and vertical gardening can also help make the most of small spaces.

Tip: Start small with easy-to-grow crops like herbs or leafy greens. Gardening can be a fun and educational way to connect with your food and become more conscious of where it comes from.

7. Choose Eco-Friendly Food Packaging

The packaging of our food is another area where we can make more sustainable choices. Single-use plastic packaging contributes significantly to plastic pollution, especially when it comes to processed foods. Look for products that use minimal, recyclable, or biodegradable packaging.

Many companies are now offering bulk options, which allow you to buy products without the wasteful packaging. Bringing your own reusable bags, jars, or containers when shopping

can further reduce your plastic consumption.

Tip: Whenever possible, buy bulk or loose items that don't

require packaging. Bring your own containers to the store for

items like grains, nuts, or deli meat.

Sustainable Eating for a Healthier Planet

Making greener food choices is a powerful way to reduce your environmental footprint while improving your health and supporting ethical practices. By eating more plant-based meals, buying locally grown and organic produce, reducing food waste, and supporting sustainable agriculture, we can all contribute to a more sustainable food system.

The transition to a greener diet doesn't require radical changes—it's about making thoughtful choices, one meal at a time. As we embrace more sustainable eating habits, we not only protect the planet but also foster a healthier, more resilient food system for generations to come.

Every meal is an opportunity to make a positive impact. By being mindful of what we eat, where it comes from, and how it's produced, we can create a food system that is more sustainable, equitable, and nourishing for all.

Chapter 7: Sustainable Transportation

The Environmental Impact of Transportation

Transportation is a key contributor to global greenhouse gas emissions. In fact, it accounts for nearly a quarter of global carbon dioxide emissions, with road transport being the largest single source. This includes emissions from cars, trucks, buses, and motorcycles, as well as the energy-intensive processes involved in manufacturing vehicles. The use of fossil fuels in conventional vehicles not only contributes to air pollution but also exacerbates climate change, as these emissions are a major driver of global warming.

In addition to the direct emissions from vehicles, transportation infrastructure itself can have significant environmental impacts. Roads, highways, and airports often require extensive land use and lead to habitat destruction and fragmentation, contributing to biodiversity loss. The production and maintenance of roads, vehicles, and airports also consume large amounts of resources and energy.

However, transportation is essential to modern life, so the goal

is not to eliminate it altogether, but to make it more

sustainable. By shifting our transportation choices to greener

alternatives, we can significantly reduce our carbon footprint

and help mitigate the environmental impact of travel.

The Benefits of Sustainable Transportation

Adopting sustainable transportation practices offers a range of benefits, both for the environment and for individuals. Some of the key advantages include:

- **Reduced greenhouse gas emissions:** By shifting away from fossil fuel-powered transportation and opting for low-emission or zero-emission alternatives, we can help reduce the overall carbon footprint of transportation.

- **Improved air quality:** Sustainable transportation choices, such as electric vehicles (EVs) and public transportation, help reduce air pollution, which is particularly important for improving public health in urban areas.

- **Cost savings:** Many green transportation options, such as biking, walking, and using public transportation, can save money on gas, parking, and vehicle maintenance.

- **Reduced congestion and land use:** By promoting public transportation, biking, and walking, we can reduce traffic congestion and the need for extensive road networks, freeing up space for parks, green spaces, and more sustainable urban development.

Sustainable Transportation Options

There are numerous ways to reduce the environmental impact of transportation. Whether you're commuting to work, running errands, or going on a road trip, there are greener alternatives to traditional car travel. Here are some sustainable transportation options that can help reduce your carbon footprint:

1. Electric Vehicles (EVs)

Electric vehicles are a cleaner, more sustainable alternative to conventional gasoline-powered cars. Unlike traditional vehicles, EVs produce zero tailpipe emissions, which means they do not release carbon dioxide, nitrogen oxides, or particulate matter into the atmosphere. The production of electricity to charge EVs can still have an environmental impact, but as the grid becomes increasingly powered by renewable energy, the carbon footprint of EVs continues to decrease.

In addition to their environmental benefits, EVs often have lower operating costs compared to conventional cars. They require less maintenance, as they have fewer moving parts, and the cost of electricity is generally cheaper than gasoline.

Tip: If you're considering an EV, check if there are any government incentives or rebates available in your area to help offset the initial purchase cost. Also, make sure to choose an EV with a range that suits your driving habits.

2. Public Transportation

Public transportation—such as buses, trains, and subways—offers a highly efficient and environmentally friendly way to travel, particularly in urban areas. By taking public transportation, you reduce the number of cars on the road, which helps decrease traffic congestion, reduce emissions, and lower energy consumption. Public transit is also more energy-efficient than private vehicles, as it can carry many passengers at once, reducing the per capita energy usage.

Most cities around the world have extensive public transit networks, and many are expanding and improving their services to make them more efficient, accessible, and environmentally friendly.

Tip: Consider using public transportation whenever possible, especially for short trips. Many cities now offer mobile apps that make it easier to plan routes and track schedules, making public transit a convenient and affordable option.

3. Biking

Biking is one of the most eco-friendly modes of transportation. Not only is it carbon-free, but it's also a great way to stay active and improve your health. Cycling eliminates the need for fuel, reduces traffic congestion, and helps reduce air pollution. It also takes up far less space than cars, reducing the environmental impact of infrastructure like parking lots and roadways.

Many cities around the world have invested in bike lanes, bike-sharing programs, and bike-friendly policies, making it easier and safer to cycle. Whether you're commuting to work, running errands, or simply getting some exercise, biking is a low-cost, low-impact option that can be part of your everyday routine.

Tip: If biking long distances or commuting is not feasible for you, consider using a hybrid option like an electric bike, which can give you a boost on longer rides while still reducing your reliance on fossil fuels.

4. Walking

Perhaps the most sustainable transportation option is walking. It's zero-emission, it costs nothing, and it has a wide range of health benefits. Walking is the perfect choice for short trips—whether it's to the store, to a friend's house, or to a nearby park. By walking instead of driving, you eliminate the need for a car altogether, reducing your carbon footprint and promoting a healthier lifestyle.

Walking also helps reduce traffic congestion and promotes the development of pedestrian-friendly infrastructure, which benefits the community by creating safer, more walkable spaces.

Tip: Take the opportunity to walk more often, especially for short trips. If your city has pedestrian-friendly infrastructure, walking can be a faster and more enjoyable option than driving.

5. Carpooling and Ride-Sharing

For longer trips where public transportation or cycling isn't an option, carpooling and ride-sharing are great alternatives to single-occupancy vehicle travel. By sharing a ride with others, you can reduce the number of cars on the road, decrease traffic congestion, and lower your overall emissions. Ride-sharing services like Uber and Lyft also offer carpooling options, which can further reduce the environmental impact of travel.

In addition to the environmental benefits, carpooling can save you money on fuel, parking, and tolls. It also fosters a sense of community and can be a more enjoyable way to travel.

Tip: Use carpooling apps or coordinate with friends, neighbors, or coworkers to share rides. Many apps allow you to find and join carpool groups based on your location and travel route.

6. Green Road Trips

If you must travel by car, there are several ways to make your road trips more sustainable. One of the best ways is to choose a fuel-efficient or electric vehicle, which will help reduce your carbon emissions over long distances. You can also reduce your fuel consumption by maintaining proper tire pressure, avoiding excessive idling, and driving at moderate speeds.

Planning your route efficiently can also reduce your environmental impact. Avoiding traffic, reducing unnecessary detours, and combining multiple errands or trips into one can help minimize fuel consumption and emissions.

Tip: If you're planning a road trip, consider renting an electric vehicle or hybrid car to reduce your environmental impact. Many car rental agencies now offer these options, and they can be a great choice for long-distance travel.

The Future of Sustainable Transportation

As cities and governments around the world become more focused on sustainability, the future of transportation looks increasingly green. Advances in electric vehicle technology, improvements to public transportation infrastructure, and the rise of autonomous vehicles all promise to make transportation cleaner, more efficient, and more accessible.

Many cities are also investing in "smart transportation" systems, which integrate real-time data and technology to optimize traffic flow, improve public transit, and reduce emissions. As the demand for sustainable transportation options grows, we are likely to see even more innovation in this area.

Tip: Stay informed about the latest developments in green transportation. As more options become available, there will be new opportunities to reduce your environmental footprint and embrace more sustainable modes of travel.

Driving Towards a Greener Future

Sustainable transportation is an essential part of a sustainable lifestyle. By choosing low-emission, energy-efficient modes of travel, we can reduce our carbon footprint, conserve resources, and help mitigate climate change. Whether it's through walking, biking, using public transportation, or driving an electric vehicle, there are many ways to make transportation more eco-friendly.

The transition to greener transportation requires changes at the individual, community, and governmental levels. However, by making conscious choices in our daily travel, we can contribute to a cleaner, healthier planet and create a transportation system that works for everyone. Each step we take toward sustainable transportation brings us closer to a future where mobility is both efficient and environmentally responsible.

Chapter 8: Green Home Design and DIY Projects

The Environmental Impact of Home Building and Renovation

The process of building or renovating a home can be resource-intensive and damaging to the environment if traditional materials and methods are used. Conventional construction materials such as concrete, steel, and plastic require significant energy to produce and often involve the extraction of raw materials from the earth, leading to habitat destruction and resource depletion. Additionally, the construction industry generates a large amount of waste, much of which ends up in landfills.

The good news is that sustainable building practices are gaining traction, and homeowners are increasingly opting for green design and renovation methods that prioritize energy efficiency, sustainable materials, and eco-friendly construction techniques. By making conscious decisions during the design, construction, and renovation phases of homeownership, we can reduce our environmental footprint,

conserve resources, and create healthier living spaces.

The Benefits of Green Home Design

A green home is designed with sustainability in mind. The benefits of green home design go beyond environmental impact—they also include financial savings, improved health, and increased comfort. Here are some of the key advantages of building or renovating a green home:

- **Energy efficiency:** Green homes are designed to reduce energy consumption, which lowers utility bills and reduces greenhouse gas emissions.

- **Resource conservation:** Sustainable homes use materials that are renewable, recyclable, or made from recycled content, helping to conserve natural resources and reduce waste.

- **Healthier living environments:** Green homes often feature non-toxic materials, better indoor air quality, and natural light, which can improve physical and mental well-being.

- **Increased property value:** Homes built or renovated with sustainable features often have higher resale values, as many buyers prioritize energy efficiency and eco-friendly features.

Creating a green home requires careful planning and consideration of every aspect, from the materials used in construction to the systems that power and maintain the home. The good news is that many green home design features can be incorporated into any type of home, whether you're building from scratch or renovating an existing space.

Key Principles of Green Home Design

Green home design focuses on creating a living space that minimizes energy consumption, reduces environmental impact, and enhances the well-being of its occupants. Here are the key principles that guide green home design:

1. Energy Efficiency

Energy-efficient homes use less energy to heat, cool, and power the home's appliances and systems. These homes are typically well-insulated, airtight, and equipped with energy-efficient appliances and lighting. Here are some strategies to improve energy efficiency in your home:

- **Proper insulation:** Insulating walls, attics, and floors helps to maintain a consistent indoor temperature and reduces the need for heating and cooling.

- **Energy-efficient windows:** Installing double or triple-pane windows helps keep heat inside during the winter and outside during the summer.

- **LED lighting:** Replacing incandescent bulbs with energy-efficient LED lights can reduce energy consumption by up to 75%.

- **Energy-efficient appliances:** Look for appliances that have the ENERGY STAR label, which indicates they meet high energy efficiency standards.

Tip: If you're renovating, consider adding spray foam insulation to seal gaps and improve energy efficiency in older homes.

2. Sustainable Building Materials

One of the most important aspects of green home design is selecting sustainable building materials that minimize environmental impact. Sustainable materials are those that are renewable, recyclable, or have a low embodied energy—meaning they require less energy to produce and transport.

Some examples of sustainable building materials include:

- **Bamboo:** A fast-growing, renewable resource that can be used for flooring, cabinetry, and furniture.

- **Reclaimed wood:** Using salvaged wood from old buildings or furniture helps reduce the need for new timber and gives new life to materials that would otherwise be discarded.

- **Recycled metal and glass:** Recycled metal and glass are durable, eco-friendly materials that can be used in countertops, flooring, and fixtures.

- **Cork:** A renewable, biodegradable material that can be used for flooring, insulation, and wall coverings.

Tip: If building from scratch, choose materials that have low embodied energy, such as reclaimed wood, cork, or natural stone, rather than resource-intensive materials like concrete or steel.

3. Water Conservation

Water conservation is another important aspect of green home design. The average household uses a significant amount of water each day, much of which is wasted through inefficient fixtures, irrigation, and leaks. Sustainable homes incorporate water-saving technologies to reduce water consumption and ensure that water is used efficiently.

Here are some ways to conserve water in your home:

- **Low-flow faucets and showerheads:** These fixtures use less water while still providing adequate pressure.

- **Water-efficient appliances:** Look for dishwashers and washing machines that use less water and energy.

- **Rainwater harvesting systems:** Installing a rainwater collection system can help capture rainwater for use in irrigation or flushing toilets.

- **Native landscaping:** Use drought-tolerant plants in your garden that require less water and maintenance.

Tip: Install a smart irrigation system that adjusts watering schedules based on weather conditions to avoid overwatering your garden.

4. Indoor Air Quality

The materials used in home construction and renovation can have a significant impact on indoor air quality. Many conventional building materials, paints, and finishes contain volatile organic compounds (VOCs) and other chemicals that can contribute to poor air quality, which can lead to health issues such as respiratory problems, headaches, and allergies.

To improve indoor air quality, consider using non-toxic paints, finishes, and sealants, and choose materials that do not emit harmful chemicals. Some tips for improving indoor air quality include:

- **Use low-VOC or zero-VOC paints and finishes.**

- **Install a ventilation system to remove indoor pollutants and bring in fresh air.**

- **Use air-purifying plants** to naturally filter out toxins and improve air quality.

- **Avoid using synthetic carpets, which can off-gas harmful chemicals. Instead, opt for wool or natural fiber rugs.**

Tip: Consider installing a heat recovery ventilation (HRV) system to continuously bring fresh air into your home while maintaining energy efficiency.

5. Passive Solar Design

Passive solar design uses the sun's energy for heating and cooling, reducing the need for artificial heating or air conditioning. By strategically placing windows, using thermal mass materials, and incorporating shading devices, passive solar homes can harness the power of the sun to regulate indoor temperatures.

Here are some passive solar strategies for your home:

- **South-facing windows:** Position windows on the south side of the home to maximize solar heat gain in the winter and reduce the need for heating.

- **Thermal mass:** Use materials like concrete or brick that absorb heat during the day and release it at night, helping to maintain a stable indoor temperature.

- **Shading:** Install awnings, pergolas, or shade trees to block the sun's heat during the summer months.

Tip: If building or renovating, work with an architect or designer who is knowledgeable about passive solar design to maximize your home's energy efficiency.

DIY Projects for a Greener Home

In addition to large-scale renovations or new constructions, there are many simple DIY projects that can make your home more sustainable. Here are some ideas for small changes that can have a big impact:

1. Make Your Own Cleaning Products

Conventional cleaning products often contain harsh chemicals that can harm the environment. Instead of buying commercial cleaners, try making your own using natural ingredients like vinegar, baking soda, and essential oils. This reduces plastic waste from cleaning product bottles and eliminates the need for harmful chemicals.

Tip: Make an all-purpose cleaner by mixing equal parts water and vinegar, and add a few drops of essential oils like lavender or lemon for a pleasant fragrance.

2. Create a Composting System

Composting is an excellent way to reduce food waste and create nutrient-rich soil for your garden. Whether you have a backyard or live in an apartment, there are composting systems that can fit your space and lifestyle.

Tip: Start a compost bin or use a countertop composting container for vegetable scraps, coffee grounds, and eggshells. If you have a garden, use the compost to enrich your soil.

3. Install a Rain Barrel

Collecting rainwater is an easy and effective way to conserve water. A rain barrel can capture runoff from your roof and store it for use in watering your garden or washing your car.

Tip: Place your rain barrel under a downspout, and attach a hose or spigot for easy access to the water.

Creating a Sustainable Home

Green home design and DIY projects are an essential part of living sustainably. By using energy-efficient systems, sustainable materials, and water-saving technologies, we can significantly reduce our environmental impact and create healthier, more comfortable living spaces. Whether you're building a new home or renovating an existing one, every choice you make can contribute to a more sustainable and eco-friendly future.

Even small DIY projects can make a big difference in creating a greener home. From composting and making your own cleaning products to installing a rain barrel or improving indoor air quality, there are countless ways to reduce your environmental footprint. With a little creativity and effort, we can all contribute to building a more sustainable world.

Chapter 9: Eco-Friendly Travel and Vacationing

The Environmental Impact of Travel

Travel and tourism have become an integral part of modern life, providing opportunities for relaxation, exploration, and cultural exchange. However, as the industry grows, so does its environmental footprint. From air travel emissions to the strain on local ecosystems caused by over-tourism, the environmental impact of travel can be substantial.

Air travel is a significant contributor to greenhouse gas emissions. In fact, aviation accounts for approximately 2-3% of global carbon emissions, with long-haul flights having the highest impact due to their large fuel consumption. Beyond carbon emissions, tourism can also lead to the degradation of natural resources, pollution, and habitat destruction, especially in fragile ecosystems like coral reefs and rainforests.

The good news is that sustainable travel is on the rise. With a growing awareness of the environmental challenges posed by travel, many individuals and organizations are adopting eco-

friendly travel practices. Sustainable travel doesn't mean

avoiding travel altogether; it's about making mindful choices

that minimize your environmental impact while supporting

local communities and preserving natural resources.

The Benefits of Eco-Friendly Travel

Eco-friendly travel isn't just about reducing emissions or conserving resources—it's also about enhancing the overall travel experience. By adopting more sustainable practices, you can contribute to the well-being of the planet and its inhabitants while enriching your own travel experience. Here are some of the key benefits of eco-friendly travel:

- **Reduced carbon footprint:** By making greener transportation and accommodation choices, you can significantly reduce the carbon emissions associated with your trip.

- **Support for local communities:** Eco-friendly travel often involves supporting locally owned businesses, ensuring that tourism benefits local economies and fosters cultural exchange.

- **Conservation of natural resources:** Sustainable travel helps protect the natural environments and wildlife that make travel so rewarding, ensuring that future

generations can enjoy these same places.

- **Personal fulfillment:** Eco-friendly travel often

encourages deeper, more meaningful connections with

destinations, allowing you to engage more fully with

local cultures and the environment.

Sustainable Travel Options

There are many ways to reduce the environmental impact of your travel, whether you're flying halfway across the world or taking a weekend road trip. Here are some practical tips and sustainable travel options to help you travel more consciously:

1. Choose Sustainable Transportation

Transportation is one of the largest sources of carbon emissions associated with travel, so making sustainable transportation choices is a key step in reducing your environmental impact. There are several green transportation options to consider:

- **Fly less, and choose eco-friendly flights:** Air travel has a large carbon footprint, especially for long-haul flights. When possible, opt for alternative modes of transportation such as trains or buses, which typically have a lower environmental impact. If you must fly, choose direct flights, as they tend to emit fewer emissions than connecting flights.

- **Electric and hybrid vehicles:** If you're driving to your destination, consider renting an electric or hybrid car. These vehicles produce fewer emissions and are more fuel-efficient than traditional gasoline-powered cars.

- **Trains and buses:** In many parts of the world, trains and buses are eco-friendly alternatives to flying or driving. Trains are especially energy-efficient, particularly in countries with well-developed rail systems, like Europe and parts of Asia.

- **Biking and walking:** For short distances, consider using bikes or walking. These are not only eco-friendly but also allow you to experience your destination in a more personal and intimate way.

Tip: Use train or bus services for short to medium distances, and opt for electric vehicles or car-sharing programs when renting a car.

2. Stay at Eco-Friendly Accommodations

The environmental impact of where you stay can also have a significant effect on the overall sustainability of your trip. Many hotels, resorts, and hostels are adopting greener practices by using renewable energy, reducing waste, conserving water, and supporting local initiatives.

Look for accommodations that are certified with green building standards, such as LEED (Leadership in Energy and Environmental Design) or Green Key. These certifications ensure that the property follows environmentally responsible practices. Additionally, many eco-lodges and boutique hotels are committed to sustainability and support local communities by sourcing food and materials locally.

Tip: When booking accommodations, look for eco-friendly options and check if they have initiatives like recycling programs, water-saving measures, and energy-efficient systems.

3. Embrace Slow Travel

Slow travel is a growing trend that encourages travelers to take their time and immerse themselves in the culture and environment of a destination. Rather than rushing through a checklist of tourist attractions, slow travel encourages a deeper connection with the place you're visiting.

By taking longer trips and exploring destinations at a more leisurely pace, you can reduce your environmental impact by minimizing the need for multiple flights or long-distance travel. Slow travel often involves staying in one place for a longer period, allowing you to enjoy local experiences, support small businesses, and engage with the community in a meaningful way.

Tip: Instead of hopping between multiple destinations, consider spending more time in one place to reduce your carbon footprint and embrace a more relaxed and enriching travel experience.

4. Support Local and Sustainable Businesses

Sustainable travel goes hand in hand with supporting local economies. By choosing local businesses for your accommodations, meals, and activities, you contribute to the economic well-being of the community and promote responsible tourism. Look for businesses that prioritize sustainability by sourcing local, organic ingredients, reducing waste, and using eco-friendly practices.

Many eco-conscious travelers opt for local experiences, such as guided tours led by local residents or visiting locally owned restaurants and markets. Supporting businesses that promote sustainability ensures that the benefits of tourism are shared with the people who live in the area.

Tip: Eat at locally owned restaurants and shop at local markets to reduce your carbon footprint and support the local economy. Seek out businesses that are committed to environmentally friendly practices.

5. Practice Responsible Wildlife Tourism

Wildlife tourism can have a significant environmental impact if it is not conducted responsibly. Many popular wildlife experiences, such as safaris, animal tours, or marine excursions, can harm the animals or ecosystems they aim to protect. It's important to choose ethical and responsible wildlife tourism experiences that prioritize animal welfare and environmental conservation.

Look for wildlife tours or experiences that are certified by ethical organizations, such as the Global Sustainable Tourism Council (GSTC) or the Rainforest Alliance. These organizations ensure that the experiences are aligned with conservation efforts and respect the well-being of animals.

Tip: Choose wildlife tours that focus on education, conservation, and responsible behavior, and avoid activities that exploit animals for entertainment or put undue stress on the environment.

6. Pack Light and Eco-Friendly

The items you pack can also have an impact on the environment. Heavier luggage requires more energy to transport, whether you're flying, driving, or taking a train. By packing light, you can reduce your travel-related emissions and make your trip more efficient.

Additionally, consider packing eco-friendly items such as reusable water bottles, bamboo cutlery, and a cloth shopping bag to reduce the need for disposable items. When selecting toiletries, opt for products with minimal packaging or refillable containers, and avoid single-use plastic items.

Tip: Use packing cubes or bags to keep your luggage organized and avoid overpacking. Choose eco-friendly toiletries and consider using solid products like shampoo bars instead of bottled liquids.

Traveling Responsibly for a Sustainable Future

Eco-friendly travel is about making mindful choices that reduce the environmental impact of your journey while enhancing the experience for both you and the places you visit. By choosing sustainable transportation, staying in eco-friendly accommodations, supporting local businesses, and practicing responsible tourism, you can help protect the planet and its communities.

Sustainable travel is a growing movement that emphasizes the importance of conscious travel decisions. Each step you take towards greener travel—whether it's reducing your carbon emissions, supporting ethical businesses, or minimizing waste—contributes to a more sustainable and responsible tourism industry.

As the demand for eco-friendly travel options grows, more businesses and governments will be encouraged to adopt sustainable practices. By being a conscious traveler, you not only enjoy the benefits of exploring new places, but you also

help ensure that future generations can continue to do the

same.

Chapter 10: Building a Sustainable Future

The Power of Individual Action

As we look toward the future, it becomes increasingly clear that the path to a sustainable world lies in the hands of individuals. While large-scale systemic changes are necessary to address environmental challenges, the collective actions of individuals—whether small or large—have the potential to create monumental shifts. The choices we make in our daily lives, from the products we buy to the energy we use, can collectively drive demand for sustainable solutions and contribute to a greener, more equitable future.

Individual actions can inspire communities, businesses, and governments to adopt more sustainable practices. When we make conscious decisions to reduce waste, conserve energy, and support eco-friendly businesses, we send a clear message that sustainability is not a passing trend, but a necessary and urgent priority.

This chapter will explore the ways in which individuals can take action to create a sustainable future, the importance of community engagement, and how we can advocate for policy changes that support environmental stewardship. We'll also highlight the role of education and personal empowerment in fostering a more sustainable world.

How Small Actions Create Big Change

The beauty of sustainability is that it doesn't require perfection. Every small change you make—whether it's choosing to bike instead of drive, turning off lights when you leave a room, or reducing food waste—adds up over time and contributes to a larger movement. When millions of people make small, positive changes, the impact can be profound.

One of the most powerful aspects of sustainability is the ripple effect. By adopting eco-friendly habits and sharing them with others, you can inspire your family, friends, and colleagues to do the same. This ripple effect often extends beyond personal circles, influencing businesses, institutions, and local governments to prioritize sustainable practices.

Example: If you start a composting system in your home, your neighbors may take note and decide to start composting too. If you choose to support a sustainable local business, others may follow suit, creating a market demand for more eco-

conscious companies.

By embracing sustainability in your own life, you become part

of a global movement toward environmental responsibility,

and you inspire others to join the effort.

Sustainable Communities: Building a Collective Future

While individual actions are essential, creating lasting change often requires a community-wide effort. Sustainable communities are built on shared values of resource conservation, social equity, and environmental stewardship. When communities come together to adopt sustainable practices, they create a powerful force for change.

Communities can embrace sustainability in many ways, from reducing energy consumption and waste to promoting local food systems and supporting renewable energy initiatives. In fact, sustainable communities are often healthier, more resilient, and more economically viable. Communities that prioritize green spaces, clean energy, and local economies create better quality of life for their residents while protecting the environment for future generations.

Some examples of how communities are embracing sustainability include:

- **Community gardens and urban farming:** These initiatives help reduce the carbon footprint associated with food production, increase local access to healthy foods, and foster community engagement.

- **Public transportation networks:** Sustainable transportation options such as buses, trains, and bike-sharing programs help reduce individual car use, cut down on emissions, and improve air quality.

- **Zero-waste initiatives:** Many communities have adopted zero-waste policies that encourage recycling, composting, and reducing single-use plastics, creating cleaner and more sustainable environments.

- **Renewable energy adoption:** Communities are increasingly investing in solar, wind, and geothermal energy, which reduce dependence on fossil fuels and promote energy independence.

Tip: Get involved in local sustainability initiatives—whether it's organizing a clean-up event, supporting a farmers' market, or participating in a community energy project. Local action can have a profound impact on building a sustainable future.

Advocating for Policy Changes

While individual actions are powerful, meaningful change often requires policy interventions at the local, national, and global levels. Governments play a crucial role in shaping the policies that regulate industries, protect natural resources, and incentivize sustainable practices. As citizens, it is our responsibility to advocate for policies that promote environmental sustainability and social equity.

Some ways individuals can advocate for policy changes include:

- **Voting:** Support political candidates who prioritize climate action, renewable energy, and environmental protection. Use your vote to influence policies that align with your values.

- **Engaging in grassroots movements:** Participate in local environmental campaigns, whether it's

advocating for renewable energy, tree planting, or
wildlife conservation.

- **Lobbying for change:** Write to your representatives,
  participate in petitions, or join environmental
  organizations to push for laws that protect the
  environment and promote sustainable practices.

- **Supporting sustainable businesses:** Vote with your
  dollar by purchasing from companies that prioritize
  sustainability, ethical sourcing, and green
  manufacturing practices. Encourage businesses to
  adopt environmentally responsible practices by
  supporting those that do.

Tip: Stay informed about the latest sustainability-related
policy issues in your area. Join online forums, attend town hall
meetings, and participate in discussions to ensure your voice
is heard in the ongoing conversation about environmental
protection.

Education and Empowerment for a Greener World

Education is key to building a sustainable future. As individuals, we must continue to educate ourselves about the challenges facing the planet and the solutions available to address them. By staying informed, we become better equipped to make sustainable choices, support eco-friendly businesses, and advocate for policies that protect the environment.

Moreover, education empowers us to inspire others to take action. Whether it's teaching children about sustainability, sharing tips on reducing waste with friends, or leading community workshops on energy efficiency, we all have the ability to influence the attitudes and behaviors of those around us.

There are numerous resources available to help individuals deepen their knowledge of sustainability, from books and documentaries to online courses and environmental organizations. By actively seeking knowledge, we can become more conscious consumers, better advocates, and more effective agents of change.

Tip: Take time to learn more about sustainability through reading, online courses, or attending workshops. Share what you learn with others to help spread awareness and build a collective commitment to environmental stewardship.

Creating a Legacy of Sustainability

Ultimately, the goal of sustainable living is to create a legacy of environmental stewardship and social responsibility that extends beyond our own lifetimes. Every action we take today can have a lasting impact on future generations. By living sustainably, we set an example for others to follow, contributing to a future where the planet's resources are conserved, ecosystems are protected, and communities are thriving.

A sustainable future is one where people live in harmony with nature, where resource use is minimized, and where all individuals have access to the resources they need to lead healthy, fulfilling lives. It's a future where the environment is respected and preserved, not just for us, but for future generations.

Tip: Think about the legacy you want to leave. Consider how your daily actions and decisions will affect the world for years to come. By embracing sustainability, you can help create a

future where environmental protection and social equity are

prioritized.

The Path to a Sustainable Future

Building a sustainable future requires action on every level—individual, community, and governmental. Each of us has a role to play in creating a world where people and the planet thrive together. By making conscious decisions to live sustainably, advocating for policy changes, and educating others, we can collectively build a future that is healthy, equitable, and resilient.

Remember, the journey toward sustainability is not about perfection—it's about progress. Every small change you make in your daily life, from reducing waste to conserving energy, contributes to a larger movement that will shape the world for generations to come. Together, we can create a future where sustainability is not just a choice, but a way of life.

Living Sustainably for a Better Tomorrow

As we conclude this guide to eco-friendly living, it's clear that sustainability is not just a choice, but a necessity. The challenges facing our planet—climate change, resource depletion, pollution, and loss of biodiversity—are urgent and require immediate action. However, these challenges also present an incredible opportunity for individuals, businesses, and governments to create lasting positive change.

Throughout this book, we have explored a variety of topics—from reducing waste and conserving energy to sustainable food choices and green home design. Each chapter has offered actionable steps that empower you to take control of your environmental impact. The journey toward sustainability begins with small, mindful actions, but these actions have the power to ripple out and inspire change in communities, businesses, and governments.

By making conscious decisions in our daily lives, we can collectively build a more sustainable future. Whether it's choosing eco-friendly products, adopting greener transportation habits, or supporting businesses that prioritize sustainability, every choice matters. The steps we take today will determine the quality of life for future generations, and every positive change we make contributes to a healthier planet and a more just society.

The Power of Consistency and Persistence

One of the most important lessons in sustainable living is that consistency matters. It's not about being perfect; it's about making a series of small, positive changes over time. Every action, whether it's recycling, reducing energy consumption, supporting sustainable brands, or growing your own food, helps reduce your environmental footprint.

Sustainability is not a destination, but a journey—a lifelong commitment to making better choices. While the challenges ahead may seem daunting, the collective power of individuals taking small, consistent actions can lead to profound change. Together, we have the power to shape a world that values the environment, respects natural resources, and promotes the well-being of all people.

Looking Ahead: The Future of Eco-Friendly Living

The future of eco-friendly living is full of possibilities. As awareness grows and more people adopt sustainable practices, there will be even greater opportunities for innovation and progress. New technologies will emerge that help us conserve resources, reduce emissions, and create cleaner, more sustainable systems. Green energy sources, sustainable agriculture practices, and zero-waste communities will continue to evolve, creating a more resilient and sustainable world.

Governments, businesses, and individuals are already working together to create solutions that will protect our planet for future generations. As we move forward, the key is to stay engaged, informed, and proactive in making sustainability a part of our everyday lives. Whether we're advocating for policy changes, supporting sustainable innovations, or simply being mindful of our consumption, we are all contributing to the creation of a greener, healthier world.

Your Role in the Sustainable Future

You are an integral part of this movement toward a more sustainable future. Your choices—no matter how small—matter. By reducing waste, conserving energy, choosing sustainable food, and supporting eco-friendly businesses, you help create a world where environmental health and social equity are prioritized. You can be a force for good by setting an example for others, inspiring them to adopt sustainable practices, and advocating for change in your community.

Remember, sustainability is not a trend. It is a necessary shift toward a more balanced relationship with the planet. By living sustainably, you are helping to protect the environment, conserve resources, and ensure that future generations inherit a planet that can support them.

Final Thoughts: A Call to Action

The transition to an eco-friendly lifestyle is one that benefits not only the environment but also our health, our communities, and our future. By embracing sustainability in all aspects of our lives—whether it's through our energy consumption, the food we eat, the products we buy, or the way we travel—we can make a profound impact on the world around us.

As you continue your journey toward sustainable living, remember that every small step you take counts. Each time you choose to make a more sustainable decision, you contribute to a larger, global movement toward a greener future. Together, we can create a world where sustainability is not just an option, but the foundation for a better tomorrow.

Thank you for taking the first step toward living more sustainably. The future is in your hands, and the world is waiting for you to make a difference.